YOUNG
MUSICIAN
PLAYS

PIANO
AND KEYBOARDS

CONTENTS

© Aladdin Books 1992

All rights reserved

Designed and produced by
Aladdin Books Ltd

First published in
the United States in 1993
by Gloucester Press
95 Madison Avenue
New York, N.Y. 10016

Printed in Belgium

Series designer: David West
Design: Rob Hillier
Editor: Jen Green
Picture researcher: Emma Krikler
Illustrators: Ron Hayward, David West

Library of Congress
Cataloging-in-Publication Data
Blackwood, Alan, 1932-
    Piano and keyboards / by Alan
  Blackwood.
     p. cm. -- (Young musician plays)
  Includes index.
    Summary: Explores the origin and
development of the piano, discussing
how it works and guiding the
student from the first steps of
playing to more advanced
techniques.
    ISBN 0-531-17422-0
    1. Piano--Instruction and
  study--Juvenile. [1. Piano]
  I. Title. II. Series.
MT745.B5 1993
786--dc20   93-20621
                 CIP
              AC MN

PIANO
AND KEYBOARDS

ALAN BLACKWOOD

GLOUCESTER PRESS
NEW YORK • CHICAGO • LONDON • TORONTO • SYDNEY

INTRODUCING THE KEYBOARD

The keyboard, as its name implies, is a row of levers or keys placed above a wooden board. The keys sound the notes automatically, so the keyboard player does not have to worry about the pitch of the note. But, while most other musicians play only one note at a time, a keyboard player, using both hands, may have several notes to sound at once.

Keyboards do not all have the same number of keys or notes. Most pianos have eighty-eight. Other keyboards have less. But the keys are all arranged in the same way. The white notes form a continuous line. The black notes are separated by the white notes, and are arranged in groups of two or three.

C   D   E   F   G   A   B   C   D   E   F   G   A   B

HIGH AND LOW
Bats emit very high-pitched sounds. Some of the noises they produce are so high that they cannot be detected by human ears.

Whales emit very low notes, which can be heard as throbs. The deep notes of an organ are also so low that only the throb of their vibrations is audible.

Low notes vibrate more slowly.

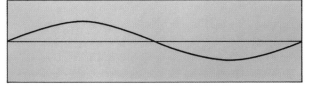

High notes vibrate more rapidly.

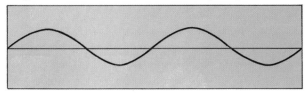

PITCH

Sounds are vibrations. The more rapid they are, the higher is the "pitch" of a sound. Putting it another way, pitch is the highness or lowness of a note. It is measured by its "frequency" – the number of vibrations per second. The notes of a keyboard, from lowest to highest, go up from hundreds to thousands of vibrations per second.

Going from left to right as you sit at the keyboard, the keys or notes (white and black together) go up in pitch by a half tone, known as a "half step."

The white notes go up by a whole tone or by a half step. The black notes go up by a tone or by a tone and a half. Try out these "pitch intervals" yourself.

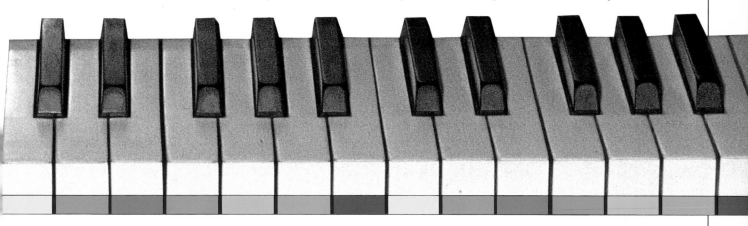

C   D   E   F   G   A   B   C   D   E   F   G   A   B

THE HYDRAULIS

The earliest type of keyboard instrument was the hydraulis, or water organ, invented around 250 B.C. The hydraulis had pipes, and a small tank of water, which kept up the pressure of air. This instrument is the ancestor of the modern grand piano.

INSIDE YOUR PIANO

The piano is a stringed instrument. Each tightly stretched set of strings (one, two, or three to a note) is a different length. The longest sound the deepest notes, and as they get shorter, the notes become higher in pitch. Each key (lever) on the keyboard operates a little soft-headed hammer that strikes its own strings, making them vibrate and sound their note.

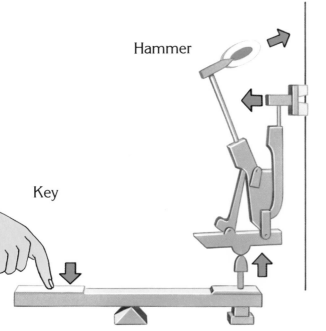

Hammer

String(s)

Damper

Key

HAMMERS
Felt-covered hammers are connected to the keys.

HOW A PIANO WORKS

The hammer mechanism is complicated. When you press a key, the hammer strikes the set of strings and bounces off again, so that the strings can vibrate. When you release the key, the damper connects with the strings and stops them from vibrating. An Italian craftsman invented the mechanism nearly 300 years ago. He called it the keyboard with "soft and loud," in Italian, *piano e forte*. That's why we call it the piano.

STRINGS
The strings, of copper or steel, are placed at an angle and across each other (overstrung) to save space, and to spread the tension of the strings across the frame.

SOUNDING BOARD
A metal sounding board amplifies the sound of the strings.

PARTS OF AN UPRIGHT PIANO

TUNING PEGS
Tuning pegs tighten or loosen the strings and keep them tuned to the right pitch.

DAMPERS
Dampers are pads that stop the strings from vibrating when the pianist takes his or her fingers off the keys.

SUSTAINING PEDAL
The "sustaining" pedal keeps the dampers off the strings, so that they vibrate longer.

SOFT PEDAL
The "soft" pedal softens the note with the dampers.

DEVELOPMENT OF THE KEYBOARD

HARPSICHORD
The harpsichord is an older type of keyboard instrument. Its strings are plucked with a plectrum instead of being struck with a hammer.

SQUARE PIANO
An old "square piano" was in fact in the shape of a rectangle, not a true square. It had a shorter keyboard, and fewer strings, than a modern piano.

GRAND PIANO
The modern concert grand is a masterpiece of construction. Smaller grand pianos are called baby grands.

GETTING DOWN TO BUSINESS

The piano is a mechanical instrument, with many moving parts. We can think of the pianist as its driver. Just as the driver of a car sits in a certain position and uses hands and feet to control the vehicle, so the pianist must sit correctly and use arms, wrists, hands, and fingers in special ways to operate his or her instrument.

Keep your back straight. It's less tiring. Don't use an ordinary chair, which would restrict your movement. If the stool is too low, use a cushion.

POSTURE
Sit facing the note called Middle C, just above the lock for the keyboard lid. Your knees should be tucked just under the edge of the keyboard – then your hands will rest on the keyboard at just about the right height and distance from the rest of your body.

HANDS AND FINGERS
Place the fingers of each hand lightly on the middle of the white notes, not on the edge, and not too close to the black notes, as they might get stuck between them. Keep your hands fairly loose at the wrists. Keep your fingers slightly arched and relaxed.

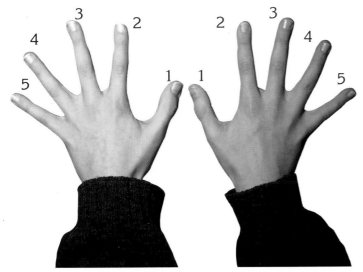

FINGERING

Fingering is about playing the notes with the most suitable fingers. It is a very important part of playing the piano. The fingers of each hand are numbered as shown. We sometimes speak of the thumb and fingers. But it is best to think of them all as a number from one to five, because that's how fingering is indicated on pieces of written music.

Middle C

FINDING MIDDLE C

Place your hands on the keyboard, with both thumbs on Middle C. The fingering of left and right hands works the opposite way around – an obvious point, but an important one.

CARING FOR YOUR PIANO

Have your piano tuned at least once a year. Keep the keys clean with a sponge or cloth moistened with warm, soapy water.

Keep a cup or bowl of water by the piano, if it is in a warm, dry room.

Don't place the piano by a radiator. The heat may crack part of the frame. Don't place your piano in strong sunlight, which would be bad for the polish or varnish.

Don't put drinks by the keyboard or on top of the piano.

PLAYING A SCALE

The word "scale" comes from the Italian word *scala*, meaning "step." Scales are steps of notes running up and down the keyboard. Playing scales is the best way to learn good fingering, and tone up the muscles in your hands.

5 4 3 2 1

1 2 3 4 5

FIVE-FINGER EXERCISE

With the left hand, start with the fifth finger on the note shown and go up five white notes to Middle C, one finger per note, and down again. With the right hand, start with the first finger (thumb) on Middle C and go up five white notes, one finger per note, and down again. Repeat this until you find it easy.

LEFT-HAND SCALE

Start with the fifth finger on the note eight white notes down from Middle C. Come up the scale one note at a time. When you reach the thumb, bring the third finger over on the next note, and complete the scale up to C.

Going up, when you reach the thumb, bring the third finger over.

1

3

2

CAMILLE SAINT-SAËNS

The French composer Camille Saint-Saëns wrote *Carnival of the Animals*, which includes pieces about elephants, a donkey, a swan, a tortoise, and fish in an aquarium. There is also a light-hearted piece called "Pianists." In it, two pianists pound up and down the keyboard, as though practicing their scales. Listen for it.

Saint-Saëns was a famous organist and pianist. As well as *Carnival of the Animals* he composed operas, symphonies, and concertos. He died in 1921, at the age of 86.

RIGHT-HAND SCALE

Start with the first finger (the thumb) on Middle C. Bring the thumb under the third finger, and complete the upward scale of eight white notes, one finger per note. Coming down, bring the third finger over the thumb to complete the scale back to C.

Here is the thumb going under the third finger as you go up the scale.

READING THE DOTS

Notation is the name given to written music. It is the equivalent of the letters and words of written language. Notation has to indicate the pitch of the notes in a piece of music (how high or low the notes are), as well as the rhythm of the music. The next pages will explore both these aspects of notated music.

NAMING THE NOTES

The pitch of notes is indicated by five lines called a staff. Whether notes are placed on, between, above, or below these lines tells us their pitch. The notes are named after the letters A to G. On the right you can see an easy way of remembering the notes on and between the lines for the left hand.

On the lines:	Between the lines:
Good Boys Deserve Fun Always.	All Cows Eat Grass.

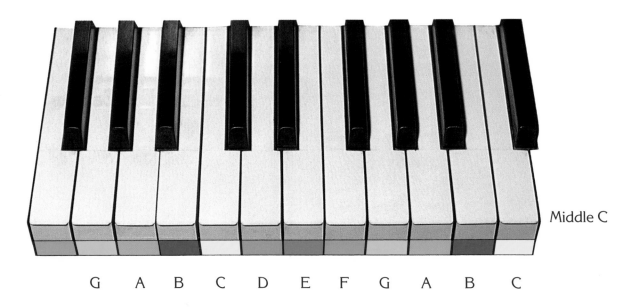

Middle C

G   A   B   C   D   E   F   G   A   B   C

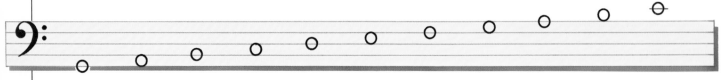

The bass clef sign (above) indicates the pitch range of the notes played by the left hand.

Above are the main notes for the left hand shown on the keyboard, and in notation.

The notes are called by the letters of the alphabet from A to G. After G the letters begin again.

THE HISTORY OF NOTATION

The system of notation we use today dates back nearly a thousand years. Early examples from the 10th and 11th centuries show staff lines, with notes written on or between them. Clef signs sometimes appear at the beginning of the music. Some early manuscripts have different symbols for notes of different lengths.

MORE NOTES TO LEARN

Here are the main notes for the right hand shown in notation, and on the keyboard, with their names as letters.

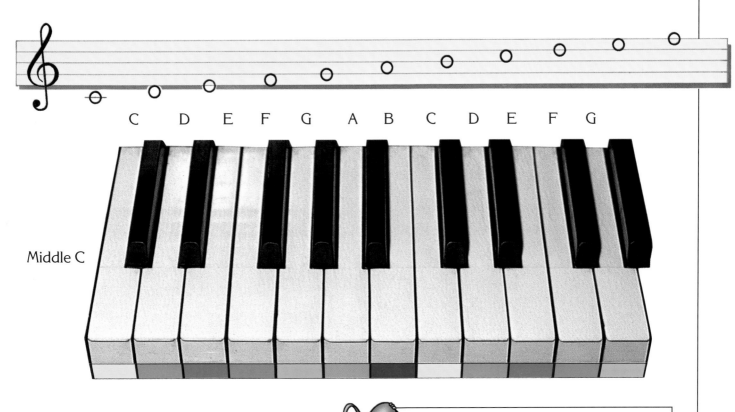

Middle C

Notice the treble clef sign this time, which indicates the pitch range of notes for the right hand to play.

Note the position of Middle C in the treble clef. Look to see where it was in the bass clef.

On the lines: Elephants Go Breaking Down Fences.

Between the lines: the names of the notes spell FACE.

On the right you can see a simple way of remembering the notes on and between the lines in the treble clef.

ADDING THE BEAT

Rhythm drives a piece of music along. Clapping your hands to music is a good way of finding its rhythm, that is, its beat. This beat is usually divided into regular sections, called bars, or measures. We speak of the rhythm of a piece of music as so many beats to the bar.

TIME VALUE OF NOTES
Notes may last for a longer or shorter time, as long as they keep to the rhythm. The note shown here that lasts longest is the whole note. Reading from left to right, each of the other notes is half the duration, or time value, of the one before.

One whole note   Two half notes   Four quarter notes

BEATS TO THE BAR
Music is divided into bars or measures. The number and value of the beats in each bar is the time signature, which appears beside the clef sign. 4/4 time has four quarter notes to every bar, or the equivalent made up in notes of other time values.

TEMPO
Tempo means the pace, or speed, of the music, as distinct from its rhythm. Common tempo indications, which are all Italian words, are *adagio* (slow), *andante* (fairly slow), *allegro* (fast) and *presto* (very fast). These directions appear at the beginning of the piece of music.

See how the notes fit into rhythms of so many beats to each bar.

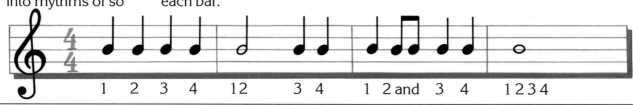

MORE TIME SIGNATURES

3/4 time and 6/8 time are two other time signatures which are often used in music. 3/4 time has three quarter notes to every bar, or the equivalent in other notes. 6/8 time has six eighth notes to every bar, or the equivalent.

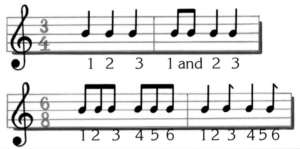

Try clapping to rhythms above.

Eight eighth-notes

RHYTHM AND DANCE

The waltz, in 3/4 rhythm, is the most popular dance of all time. It began in Germany and Austria about 170 years ago. One of the most successful composers of waltzes was Johann Strauss II. Strauss lived in Vienna and wrote many popular waltzes, such as "The Blue Danube" and "Tales from the Vienna Woods."

Rock and roll is in 4/4 rhythm. It started in the 1950s as a kind of up tempo, speeded-up blues (see page 25). Elvis Presley was one of its greatest stars. Much of today's rock music is based on rock and roll.

MORE EXERCISES

On pages 10-11, you played a scale of eight notes (an octave) in both hands. Scales are one kind of exercise for practicing fingering and for strengthening fingers, hands, and wrists. Other kinds of exercises also strengthen the same muscles. This page has some exercises you can try.

BROKEN CHORDS

Broken chords involve playing the notes of chords as individual notes. This exercise stretches your fingers and gets you used to playing notes that are farther apart on the keyboard.

Here is the notation for a sequence of broken chords for the left hand. Follow the fingering below.

On the opposite page you can see the same sequence of notes for the right hand to play.

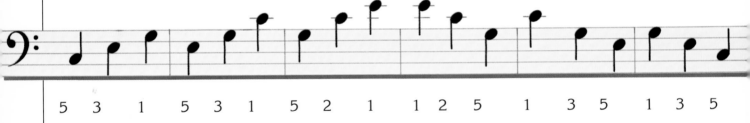

5 3 1   5 3 1   5 2 1   1 2 5   1 3 5   1 3 5

PLAYING CHORDS

Chords are two or more notes of different pitch sounded together. Try these chords of three notes: two for

the left hand and two for the right. The notes are shown on the keyboard and in the notation.

16

CHROMATIC SCALE

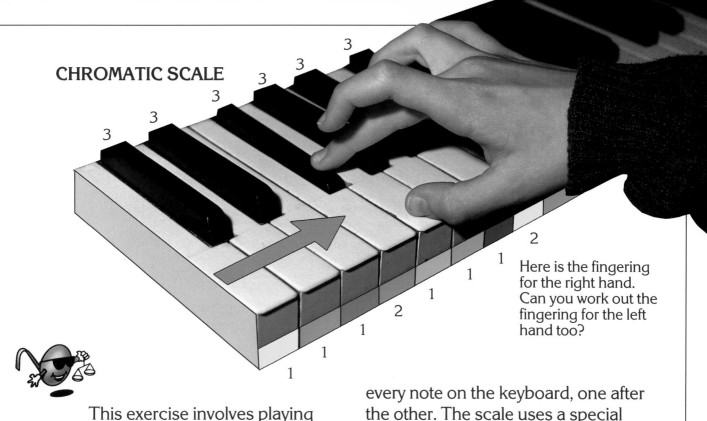

Here is the fingering for the right hand. Can you work out the fingering for the left hand too?

This exercise involves playing black notes as well as white ones, for in the chromatic scale you must play every note on the keyboard, one after the other. The scale uses a special fingering, with only the thumb (no 1) and the next two fingers (2 and 3).

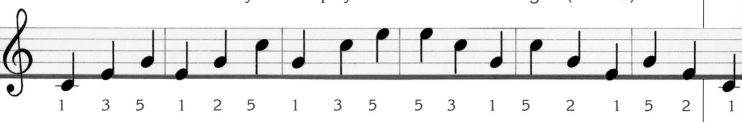

| 1 | 3 | 5 | 1 | 2 | 5 | 1 | 3 | 5 | 5 | 3 | 1 | 5 | 2 | 1 | 5 | 2 | 1 |

FRANZ LISZT

The most famous pianist of all time was the Hungarian Franz Liszt (1811–86). As a young man Liszt was very good looking, and when he started to play, young women sometimes fainted or screamed, as some fans do at rock concerts today. During Liszt's long life, pianos were made bigger and stronger, which inspired him to write a new kind of piano music. Much of this is extremely difficult to play. Listen to Liszt's *Hungarian Rhapsodies*, his exciting arrangements of old Hungarian gypsy songs and dances, and to his famous *Liebestraum* (or *Dream of Love*).

INTRODUCING SHARPS AND FLATS

The scale of eight white notes you played on pages 10-11 started and ended on the note C. It was the scale of C major. To play the same kind of scale starting and ending on a different note is more complicated. These pages introduce the scale of G major, for left and right hands. The fingering is the same as for the scale of C.

G MAJOR IN THE LEFT HAND

Below are the notes for the left hand, going up. Notice the sharp sign on the staff line for the note F.

Instead of playing the white note F, play the adjacent black note of F sharp.

5	4	3	2	1	3	2	1
G	A	B	C	D	E	F#	G

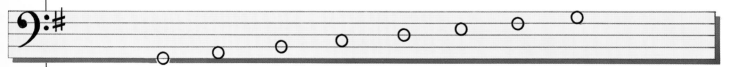

KEY SIGNATURES
The F# in the "key signature" near the clef tells you the key is G. The sharp is not marked again in the music.

SHARPS AND FLATS
The sharp sign (#) tells you to raise the pitch of a note by a half-tone. The flat sign (♭) tells you to lower the pitch of a note by a half-tone.

G MAJOR IN THE RIGHT HAND

Here is the same scale for the right hand, going up. Once again, notice the position of the sharp sign, on the staff line for the note F (this time in the treble clef). The sign tells you to play the note F sharp. As in the left hand, the fingering is the same as for the scale of C major, up and down.

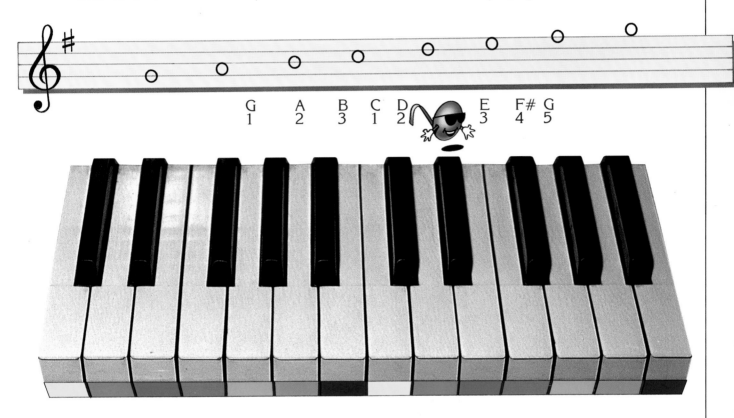

FREDERIC CHOPIN

Frederic Chopin (1810–49) wrote a piano piece known as the "Black Key Etude," because the right-hand part is all on the black notes. A study (in French *etude*) is a piece intended as an exercise, though Chopin's piano studies are also beautiful pieces of music. Chopin, who was Polish, was both a great pianist and a great composer of piano music. Several other pieces by Chopin have popular nicknames, including the "Raindrop Prelude," the "Minute Waltz," the "Winter Wind Etude," and the "Butterfly Etude."

MAJOR AND MINOR

You have already met the scales of C major and G major. You can play a major scale starting on any of the white or black notes (depending on how many sharps or flats are included). Minor scales are organized in a different way, and have quite a different sound to them.

A MINOR

Minor scales can also start and end on any of the white and black notes. Below is the notation and fingering for the scale of A minor for the left and right hands going up and down. You'll see that the treble clef part appears above the bass clef part. This is the normal order for the right- and left-hand parts in written music.

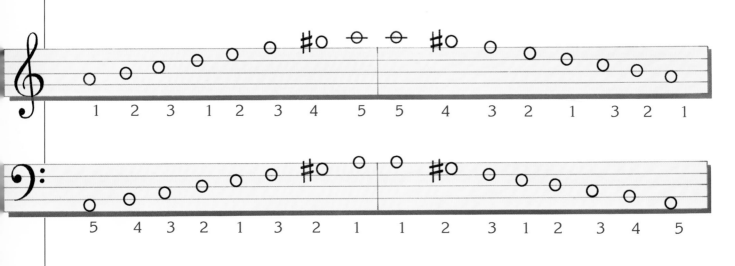

In this scale the note G is "accidentally" sharpened (see page 21). You must play G sharp every time you come to it.

The "soft" and "sustaining" pedals are used to make the piano sound softer or louder, or sustain (hold onto) notes.

ACCIDENTALS

Accidentals are any notes that are sharpened or flattened, in addition to the sharps or flats that are indicated in the key signature. In the scale of A minor, the note G is "accidentally" sharpened. And in the scale of E minor (below) the note D is "accidentally" sharpened – in addition to the note F, which is already sharpened by the key signature.

NATURALS

The "natural" sign (shown on the right) looks quite like the sign for a sharp. But beware, this sign means that the instruction to sharpen or flatten a note has been canceled. If the note F has been sharpened, but the composer now wants you to play the white note F, he puts a natural sign beside it. You must play F natural, not F sharp.

E MINOR

Here is the notation for the scale of E minor for the left and right hands going up and down. Notice the F sharp in the key signature. The fingering is the same for this scale as for the other scales you have met.

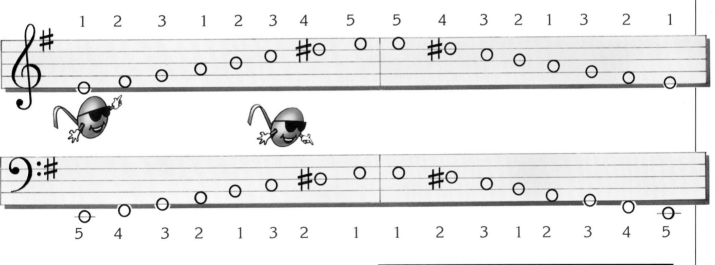

The note F has been sharpened in the key signature. Play F sharp every time you come to it.

The note D is "accidentally" sharpened. Play D sharp every time you come to it.

The note F has been sharpened in the key signature. Play F sharp every time you come to it.

Japanese pianist Mitsuko Uchida is renowned for her performances today.

PLAYING MELODIES

Now you are ready to play some real melodies. These two pieces are written in the treble clef, because it is usually the right hand that plays the melody in piano music. New points about notation are explained on the opposite page.

ODE TO JOY

3   4 5   5 4 3 2   1   2 3

3 2   3   4 5   5 4 3 2

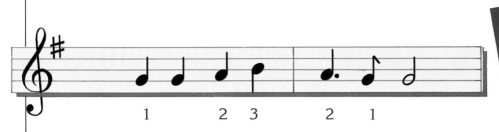

1   2 3   2 1

The German composer Ludwig van Beethoven (1770–1827) wrote dramatic and exciting piano music.

The "Ode to Joy" is the melody from the last movement of Beethoven's Ninth ("Choral") Symphony. It is the national anthem of the European Community. This arrangement is in G major, with F sharp in the key signature.

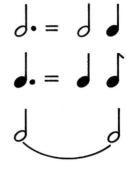

RESTS

A rest is a silent beat in a bar of music. Different rest symbols correspond to the different kinds of notes, and show how long the silence should be.

whole note   half note

quarter note   eighth note

DOTTED NOTES AND TIES

A dot after a note increases the time value of the note by a half. A tie connects two notes of the same pitch. Play them as one long note.

PLAISIR D'AMOUR

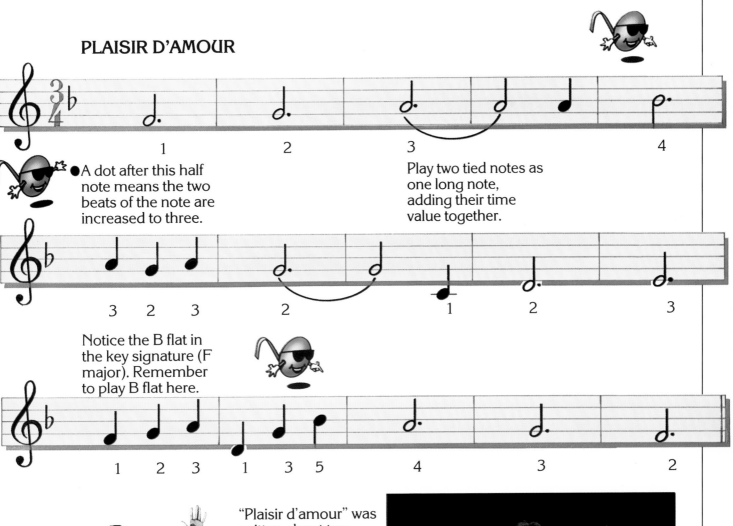

1   2   3   4

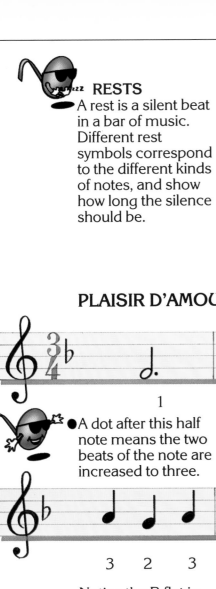

A dot after this half note means the two beats of the note are increased to three.

Play two tied notes as one long note, adding their time value together.

3   2   3   2   1   2   3

Notice the B flat in the key signature (F major). Remember to play B flat here.

1   2   3   1   3   5   4   3   2

"Plaisir d'amour" was written about two hundred years ago by Martini il Tedesco (Martini the German). Elvis Presley and folk-singer Joan Baez have both sung versions of it. This arrangement is in the key of F major (with a B flat in the key signature).

BOTH HANDS NOW

Now is the time to play a piece with both hands. Practice the parts separately before you try to play them together. Later you will be able to read and play both the right- and left-hand parts at the same time.

GREENSLEEVES

5 2 1   5 2 1   (throughout)

GREENSLEEVES

The old English folk song "Green-sleeves" dates back to the time of Shakespeare, or even earlier. It is an early love ballad — a form still popular among musicians today, including keyboard player Stevie Wonder (right). This arrangement is in the key of A minor, with no sharps or flats in the key signature; but there are some accidental sharps. The rhythm has been simplified slightly.

TWELVE-BAR BLUES

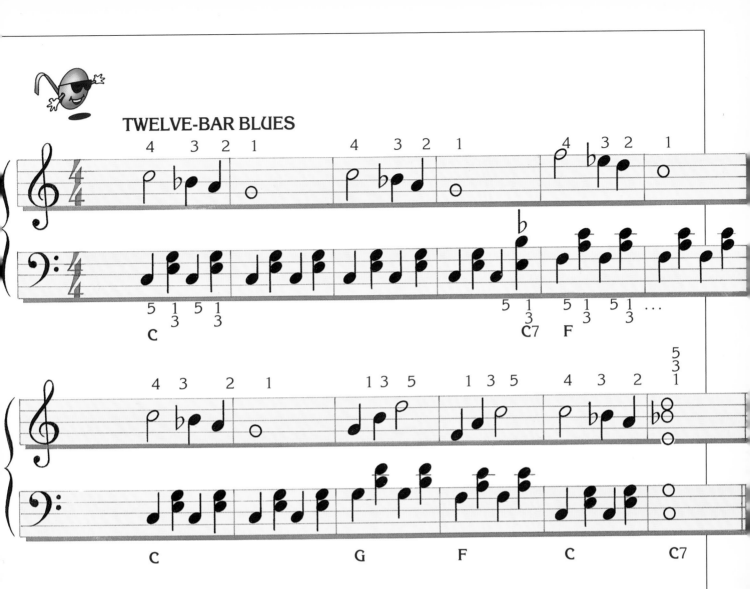

THE BLUES

Blues was originally a kind of folk music that originated among American black people. The twelve-bar blues is the classic form. Much of the music of jazz, leading to rock and roll, started with the blues. The American composer and musician W.C. Handy (right) is often called the "father of the blues." He wrote the famous "St. Louis Blues" and "Basin Street Blues."

TWELVE-BAR BLUES

Notice the accidental flat notes in the piece above. The rhythm of the melody has been kept simple; see if you can "jazz it up" a bit. You'll see, too, that chord symbols have been added. These are great fun; ask in your library or in a music store for a book showing how they work.

THE WORLD OF THE PIANO

The piano is the most popular of all instruments, because it can play melody and harmonies together. More people play the piano than any other instrument, and more well-known music has been written for the piano than for any other instrument. The piano is also very versatile – you can see some of its many roles on these pages.

PIANO AND ORCHESTRA

The use of the piano as an instrument in the orchestra dates back to the beginning of the twentieth century. Before that, the piano was used as a concerto instrument only. (A concerto is a composition for a solo instrument and orchestra.) The composer Igor Stravinsky was one of the first to use the piano in the orchestra, and other composers have followed his example.

PIANO QUARTET

The piano is perhaps best known as a solo or concerto instrument. But great music has also been written for the piano quartet (piano plus violin, viola and cello) and for the piano trio (piano plus violin and cello).

PLAYER PIANO

You don't have to be able to play the piano to work a player piano! This is a mechanical piano, worked by a roll of paper with thousands of little holes, or perforations, in it. It was popular in the days before records.

HONKY-TONK PIANO

Honky-tonk music is played in saloons, clubs and some dance halls. Famous American boogie-woogie pianists such as Clarence "Pine Top" Smith and Charlie "Cow Cow" Davenport played in honky-tonk saloons and halls 60–70 years ago.

JAZZ PIANO

Jazz and dance bands, such as Louis Armstrong's Hot Five (right), nearly always have a piano. Two of the greatest American band leaders, "Duke" Ellington and "Count" Basie, were pianists. They conducted their bands seated at the piano.

PREPARED PIANO

The "prepared piano" was the idea of American composer and musical thinker John Cage. Cage inserted objects such as pencils and rubber bands between the strings, or placed them over the strings, to change the whole sound of the piano. He has written a "Concerto for Prepared Piano." Cage has written (or thought of) many other extraordinary pieces of music, involving the use of tape recorders, whistles, radios, and even bottles of water!

THE KEYBOARD FAMILY

The keyboard was one of the most important musical inventions. The system of scales and keys we know today is largely based on it. The keyboard has been used in a wide variety of instruments besides the piano and the older harpsichord, just some of which are shown here.

French musician Jean-Michel Jarre (above right) pioneered the use of synthesizers and electronic sounds.

ELECTRIC KEYBOARDS
Electric organs and pianos are played very like an ordinary piano, but the sounds, like those of the synthesizer, are electronic. These instruments are very popular with jazz musicians and pop groups.

ELECTRIC ORGAN
Electric organs began to appear in movies and theaters in the 1920s. They were technically very advanced for their time, and could produce many extraordinary sounds. Visually these organs made a dramatic impact on audiences, as they rose up from the pit in front of the screen or stage during intervals in performances, with their many lights flashing.

SYNTHESIZER
Synthesizers (above) generate electronic signals which are fed though amplifiers and speakers. These signals can produce many different sounds.

CELESTA

The keyboard of a celesta plays a set of tuned metal bars inside the instrument. Tchaikovsky's "Dance of the Sugar Plum Fairy" is written for it.

ACCORDION

The accordion (right) is a kind of portable organ, with a keyboard down one side. Learning to play the keyboard at this angle takes a great deal of practice.

CHURCH ORGAN

A large church or concert organ (right) often has three or four keyboards (known as "manuals"), plus a pedal keyboard, which is played with the feet. There are also a variety of "stops" — knobs or handles that the organist pulls out or pushes in to select whole groups or sets of pipes. All these devices are needed because many organs have a large number of pipes, with a range of different sound qualities, as well as notes of different pitch. Electric organs which were used in movies or theaters are now sometimes used in churches. The organ shown on the opposite page is reused in this way.

COMPOSERS AND PERFORMERS

The history of keyboard music dates back to the time of the hydraulis (see page 5). But the great age of keyboard music, first for the harpsichord and then for the piano, began during the Renaissance – the age of Leonardo da Vinci, Shakespeare, and Galileo. Keyboard music has been flourishing ever since.

J. S. Bach

W. A. Mozart

Claude Debussy

George Gershwin

The Renaissance period, between 1400 and 1600, saw the beginning of the great age of keyboard music. Two of the first composers of keyboard music, the Englishmen **William Byrd** (1543–1623) and **Thomas Morley** (1557–1602), lived during this time. They composed for the virginal, **a** stringed keyboard instrument similar to the harpsichord.

The baroque period, from about 1600 to 1750, is noted mainly for its grand singing in opera and oratorios, and for music written for orchestras of violins. **Johann Sebastian Bach** (1685–1750) in Germany wrote music for the harpsichord. His fugues (pieces in which the notes of a theme follow themselves up and down the keyboard) are particularly famous. Bach was a choirmaster and church organist, and he also wrote music for the organ, including "chorales," based on old German hymn tunes. **François Couperin** (1668–1733) in France and

Domenico Scarlatti (1685–1757) in Italy also composed music for harpsichord and organ. Today this music is often played on the piano.

The classical period, from about 1750 to 1800, is named after the well-planned and orderly style of its music. In Austria, **Franz-Joseph Haydn** (1732–1809) and **Wolfgang Amadeus Mozart** (1756–91) wrote sonatas and other music for harpsichord or piano. Mozart could play the harpsichord at the age of three,

and gave concerts all over Europe. Later he wrote the first great piano concertos. The German composer **Ludwig van Beethoven** (1770–1827) wrote many powerful and dramatic concertos and sonatas for the piano. From the age of 30 Beethoven's hearing began to fail, and some of his greatest works were composed when he was deaf.

Beethoven carried music forward into **the Romantic period**, from 1800 to 1900.

During this time composers filled their music with passion. Many of them were great pianists as well as composers. **Franz Schubert** (1797–1828), **Robert Schumann** (1810–56), **Felix Mendelssohn** (1809–47), **Franz Liszt** (1811–86), and **Johannes Brahms** (1833–97), all came

Scott Joplin

from Germany and Austria. In France, Polish-born **Frederic Chopin** (1810–49) wrote nearly all his music for solo piano. Pianos became bigger and better during the Romantic period.

By **the modern period** (from 1900) grand pianos had a beautiful sound and touch. **Claude Debussy** (1862–1918) and **Maurice Ravel** (1875–1937) were both inspired by this. These French composer-pianists created musical "impressions" of natural phenomena like rain, sunlight, wind, and snow.

American pianist and songwriter **George Gershwin** (1898–1937) was inspired by the rhythms and harmonies of the new dance music, jazz. His famous *Rhapsody in Blue* is a kind of jazz concerto for piano and orchestra.

Alfred Brendel

Jazz was the music of black Americans; throughout this century it has inspired many brilliant, mostly black, pianists. **Scott Joplin** (1868–1917) is remembered for his piano pieces, called "rags." Other great jazz pianists include **Ferdinand "Jelly Roll" Morton, Thomas "Fats" Waller**, and the fabulous **Art Tatum** (who was nearly blind). Many concert pianists are renowned for their performances today. **Alfred Brendel** from Austria is one.

GLOSSARY

accidental a sharp or flat especially added to a piece of music.

blues a basic jazz style, often a song.

boogie speeded-up blues, often for the piano.

chord two or more notes of different pitch sounded together.

clef a sign indicating the pitch of notes in musical notation.

concerto a composition for solo instrument and orchestra.

dotted note indicates that the time value of the note is increased by half.

flat a note that is lowered in pitch by a half step.

frequency the scientific measurement of pitch.

key one of the levers on the piano which causes a note to sound; also, indication of a major or minor scale.

natural a note not sharpened or flattened.

pitch the highness or lowness of a note.

rest a silent beat in the rhythm of a piece of music.

rock and roll a dance style based on boogie-woogie.

sharp a note that is raised in pitch by a half step.

sonata a composition, often for solo piano.

staff the horizontal lines used in musical notation.

tie a line indicating that two notes of the same pitch are played as one.

Index

Photocredits
Cover and pages 4 top, 5 top, 8 both, 9 all, 10, 11 bottom, 12, 13 both, 16, 17, 18, 19 top and 20 bottom: Roger Vlitos; page 4 bottom left: Frank Lane Picture Agency; pages 4 bottom right, 5 bottom right, 14-15, 21, 23 right, 28-29 top, 28 middle, 29 bottom and 31 right: Frank Spooner Pictures; pages 5 bottom left, 7 top, 11 top, 15 bottom left, 17 bottom right, 19 bottom right, 20 top, 22 left, 27 top and 30, pictures 1, 2 and 3: Mary Evans Picture Library; page 7 bottom, 15 bottom right, 17 bottom left, 19 bottom left, 25, 27 middle right, 27 bottom, 28 bottom, 29 top and 30, picture 4: The Hulton Picture Company; page 22 right: Paul Nightingale; page 23 left: Aladdin's Lamp; page 26 top: British Broadcasting Corporation; page 26 bottom: Topham Picture Source; pages 27 middle left and 29 middle: Spectrum Colour Library; page 31 left: Redferns.